Verses

Hilaire Belloc

Alpha Editions

This edition published in 2024

ISBN : 9789362928924

Design and Setting By
Alpha Editions
www.alphaedis.com
Email - info@alphaedis.com

Contents

INTRODUCTION

By Joyce Kilmer

Far from the poets being astray in prose-writing (said Francis Thompson) it might plausibly be contended that English prose, as an art, is but a secondary stream of the Pierian fount, and owes its very origin to the poets. The first writer one remembers with whom prose became an art was Sir Philip Sidney. And Sidney was a poet.

This quotation is relevant to a consideration of Hilaire Belloc, because Belloc is a poet who happens to be known chiefly for his prose. His *Danton* and *Robespierre* have been read by every intelligent student of French history, his *Path to Rome*, that most high-spirited and engaging of travel books, has passed through many editions, his political writings are known to all lovers—and many foes—of democracy, his whimsically imaginative novels have their large and appreciative audience, and his exquisite brief essays are contemporary classics. And since the unforgetable month of August of the unforgetable year 1914, Hilaire Belloc has added to the number of his friends many thousands who care little for *belles lettres* and less for the French Revolution—he has become certainly the most popular, and by general opinion the shrewdest and best informed, of all chroniclers and critics of the Great War.

There is nothing, it may be said, about these achievements to indicate the poet. How can this most public of publicists woo the shy and exacting Muse? His superabundant energy may now and again overflow in little lyrical rivulets, but how can he find time to turn it into the deep channels of song?

Well, what is the difference between a poet who writes prose and a prose-writer who writes verse? The difference is easy to see but hard to describe. Mr. Thomas Hardy is a prose writer. He has forsaken the novel, of which he was so distinguished a master, to make cynical little sonnet portraits and to pour the acid wine of his philosophy—a sort of perverted Presbyterianism—into the graceful amphora of poetic drama. But he is not a poet. Thackeray was a prose-writer, in spite of his delicious light verse. Every novelist writes or has written verse, but not all of them are poets.

Of course, Sir Walter Scott was first of all a poet—the greatest poet who ever wrote a novel. And no one who has read *Love in the Valley* can hesitate to give Meredith his proper title. Was Macaulay a poet? I think so—but perhaps I am in a hopeless minority in my belief that the author of *The Battle of Naseby* and *The Lays of Ancient Rome* was the last of the great English ballad makers.

But this general truth cannot, I think, honestly be denied; there have been many great poets who have devoted most of their lives to writing prose. Some of them have died without discovering their neglected talent. I think that Walter Pater was one of these; much that is annoyingly subtle or annoyingly elaborate in his essays needs only rhyme and rhythm—the lovely accidents of poetry—to become graceful and appropriate. His famous description of the Mona Lisa is worthless if considered as a piece of serious æsthetic criticism. But it would make an admirable sonnet. And it is significant that Walter Pater's two greatest pupils—Lionel Johnson and Father Gerard Hopkins, S.J.,—found expression for their genius not in prose, the chosen medium of their "unforgetably most gracious friend," but in verse.

From Walter Pater, that exquisite of letters, to the robust Hilaire Belloc may seem a long journey. But there is, I insist, this similarity between these contrasting writers, both are poets, and both are known to fame by their prose.

For proof that Walter Pater was a poet, it is necessary only to read his *Renaissance Studies* or his interpretations—unsound but fascinating—of the soul of ancient Greece. Often his essays, too delicately accurate in phrasing or too heavily laden with golden rhetoric, seem almost to cry aloud for the relief of rhyme and rhythm.

Now, Hilaire Belloc suggests in many of his prose sketches that he is not using his true medium. I remember a brief essay on sleep which appeared in *The New Witness*—or, as it was then called, *The Eye Witness*—several years ago, which was not so much a complete work in itself as it was a draft for a poem. It had the economy of phrase, the concentration of idea, which is proper to poetry.

But it is not necessary in the case of Hilaire Belloc, as it is in that of Walter Pater, to search pages of prose for proof that their author is a poet. Now and then—all too seldom—the idea in this man's brain has insisted on its right, has scorned the proffered dress of prose, however fine of warp and woof, however stiff with rich verbal embroidery, and has demanded its rhymed and rhythmed wedding garments. Therefore, for proof that Hilaire Belloc is a poet it is necessary only to read his poetry.

II

Hilaire Belloc is a poet. Also he is a Frenchman, an Englishman, an Oxford man, a Roman Catholic, a country gentleman, a soldier, a democrat, and a practical journalist. He is always all these things.

One sign that he is naturally a poet is that he is never deliberately a poet. No one can imagine him writing a poem to order—even to his own order. The poems knock at the door of his brain and demand to be let out. And he lets them out, carelessly enough, setting them comfortably down on paper simply because that is the treatment they desire. And this happens to be the way all real poetry is made.

Not that all verse makers work that way. There are men who come upon a waterfall or mountain or an emotion and say: "Aha! here is something out of which I can extract a poem!" And they sit down in front of that waterfall or mountain or emotion and think up clever things to say about it. These things they put into metrical form, and the result they fondly call a poem.

There's no harm in that. It's good exercise for the mind, and of it comes much interesting verse. But it is not the way in which the sum of the world's literature is increased.

Could anything, for example, be less studied, be more clearly marked with the stigmata of that noble spontaneity we call inspiration, than the passionate, rushing, irresistible lines "To the Balliol Men Still in Africa"? Like Gilbert K. Chesterton and many another English democrat, Hilaire Belloc deeply resented his country's war upon the Boers. Yet his heart went out to the friends of his university days who were fighting in Africa. They were fighting, he thought, in an unjust cause; but they were his friends and they were, at any rate, fighting. And so he made something that seems (like all great writing) an utterance rather than a composition; he put his love of war in general and his hatred of this war in particular, his devotion to Balliol and to the friends of his youth into one of the very few pieces of genuine poetry which the Boer War produced. Nor has any of Oxford's much-sung colleges known praise more fit than this

"House that armours a man

With the eyes of a boy and the heart of a ranger,

And a laughing way in the teeth of the world,

And a holy hunger and thirst for danger."

But perhaps a more typical example of Hilaire Belloc's wanton genius is to be found not among those poems which are, throughout, the beautiful expressions of beautiful impressions, but among those which are careless, whimsical, colloquial. There is that delightful, but somewhat exasperating *Dedicatory Ode*. Hilaire Belloc is talking—charmingly, as is his custom—to some of his friends, who had belonged, in their university days, to a youthful revolutionary organization called the Republican Club. He happens to be talking in verse, for no particular reason except that it amuses him to talk in verse. He makes a number of excellent jokes, and enjoys them very much; his Pegasus is cantering down the road at a jolly gait, when suddenly, to the amazement of the spectators, it spreads out great golden wings and flashes like a meteor across the vault of heaven! We have been laughing at the droll tragedy of the opium-smoking Uncle Paul; we have been enjoying the humorous spectacle of the contemplative freshman—and suddenly we come upon a bit of astonishingly fine poetry. Who would expect, in all this whimsical and jovial writing, to find this really great stanza?

"From quiet homes and first beginning,

Out to the undiscovered ends.

There's nothing worth the wear of winning,

But laughter and the love of friends."

Who having read these four lines, can forget them? And who but a poet could write them? But Hilaire Belloc has not forced himself into this high mood, nor does he bother to maintain it. He gaily passes on to another verse of drollery, and then, not because he wishes to bring the poem to an effective climax, but merely because it happens to be his mood, he ends the escapade he calls an Ode with eight or ten stanzas of nobly beautiful poetry.

There is something almost uncanny about the flashes of inspiration which dart out at the astonished reader of Hilaire Belloc's most frivolous verses. Let me alter a famous epigram and call his light verse a circus illuminated by lightning. There is that monumental burlesque, the Newdigate Poem—*A Prize Poem Submitted by Mr. Lambkin of Burford to the Examiners of the University of Oxford on the Prescribed Poetic Theme Set by Them in 1893, "The Benefits of the Electric Light."* It is a tremendous joke; with every line the reader echoes the author's laughter. But without the slightest warning, Hilaire Belloc passes from the rollicking burlesque to shrewd satire; he has been merrily jesting with a bladder on a stick, he suddenly draws a gleaming rapier and thrusts it into the heart of error. He makes Mr. Lambkin say:

"Life is a veil, its paths are dark and rough

Only because we do not know enough:

When Science has discovered something more

We shall be happier than we were before."

Here we find the directness and restraint which belong to really great satire. This is the materialistic theory, the religion of Science, not burlesqued, not parodied, but merely stated nakedly, without the verbal frills and furbelows with which our forward-looking leaders of popular thought are accustomed to cover its obscene absurdity. Almost these very words have been uttered in a dozen "rationalistic" pulpits I could mention, pulpits occupied by robustuous practical gentlemen with very large eyes, great favourites with the women's clubs. Their pet doctrines, their only and most offensive dogma, is not attacked, is not ridiculed; it is merely stated for them, in all kindness and simplicity. They cannot answer it, they cannot deny that it is a mercilessly fair statement of the "philosophy" that is their stock in trade. I hope that many of them will read it.

III

Hilaire Belloc was born July 27, 1870. He was educated at the Oratory School, Edgbaston, and at Balliol College, Oxford. After leaving school he served as a driver in the Eighth Regiment of French Artillery at Toul Meurthe-et-Moselle, being at that time a French citizen. Later he was naturalized as a British subject, and entered the House of Commons in 1906 as Liberal Member for South Salford. British politicians will not soon forget the motion which Hilaire Belloc introduced one day in the early Spring of 1908, the motion that the Party funds, hitherto secretly administered, be publicly audited. His vigorous and persistent campaign against the party system has placed him, with Cecil Chesterton, in the very front ranks of those to whom the democrats of Great Britain must look for leadership and inspiration. He was always a keen student of military affairs; he prophesied, long before the event, the present international conflict, describing with astonishing accuracy the details of the German invasion of Belgium and the resistance of Liège. Now he occupies a unique position among the journalists who comment upon the War, having tremendously increased the circulation of *Land and Water*, the periodical for which he writes regularly, and lecturing to a huge audience once a week on the events of the War in one of the largest of London's concert halls—Queen's Hall, where the same vast crowds that listen to the War lectures used to gather to hear the works of the foremost German composers.

IV

Hilaire Belloc, as I have said, is a Frenchman, an Englishman, an Oxford man, a country gentleman, a soldier, a democrat, and a practical journalist. In all these characters he utters his poetry. As a Frenchman, he is vivacious and gallant and quick. He has the noble English frankness, and that broad irresistible English mirthfulness which is so much more inclusive than that narrow possession, a sense of humour. Democrat though he is, there is about him something of the atmosphere of the country squire of some generations ago; it is in his heartiness, his jovial dignity, his deep love of the land. The author of *The South Country* and *Courtesy* has made Sussex his inalienable possession; he owns Sussex, as Dickens owns London, and Blackmore owns Devonshire. And he is thoroughly a soldier, a happy warrior, as brave and dextrous, no one can doubt, with a sword of steel as with a sword of words.

He has taken the most severe risk which a poet can take: he has written poems about childhood. What happened when the late Algernon Charles Swinburne bent his energies to the task of celebrating this theme? As the result of his solemn meditation on the mystery of childhood, he arrived at two conclusions, which he melodiously announced to the world. They were, first, that the face of a baby wearing a plush cap looks like a moss-rose bud in its soft sheath, and, second, that "astrolabe" rhymes with "babe." Very charming, of course, but certainly unworthy of a great poet. And upon this the obvious comment is that Swinburne was not a great poet. He took a theme terribly great and terribly simple, and about it he wrote ... something rather pretty.

Now, when a really great poet—Francis Thompson, for example—has before him such a theme as childhood, he does not spend his time making far-fetched comparisons with moss-rose buds, or hunting for words that rhyme with "babe." Childhood suggests Him Who made childhood sacred, so the poet writes *Ex Ore Infantium*, or such a poem as that which ends with the line:

"Look for me in the nurseries of Heaven."

A poet may write pleasingly about mountains, and cyclones, and battles, and the love of woman, but if he is at all timid about the verdict of posterity he should avoid the theme of childhood as he would avoid the plague. For only great poets can write about childhood poems worthy to be printed.

Hilaire Belloc has written poems about children, and they are worthy to be printed. He is never ironic when he thinks about childhood; he is gay, whimsical, with a slight suggestion of elfin cynicism, but he is direct, as a child is direct. He has written two dedicatory poems for books to be given to children; they are slight things but they are a revelation of their author's power to do what only a very few poets can do, that is, to enter into the heart and mind of the child, following that advice which has its literary as well as moral significance, to "become as a little child."

And in many of Hilaire Belloc's poems by no means intended for childish audiences there is an appealing simplicity that is genuinely and beautifully childish, something quite different from the adult and highly artificial simplicity of Professor A. E. Housman's *A Shropshire Lad*. Take that quatrain *The Early Morning*. It is as clear and cool as the time it celebrates; it is absolutely destitute of rhetorical indulgence, poetical inversions or "literary" phrasing. It is, in fact, conversation—inspired conversation, which is poetry. It might have been written by a Wordsworth not painfully self-conscious, or by a Blake whose brain was not as yet muddled with impressionistic metaphysics.

And his Christmas carols—they are fit to be sung by a chorus of children. Can any songs of the sort receive higher praise than that? Children, too, appreciate *The Birds* and *Our Lord and Our Lady*. Nor is that wonderful prayer rather flatly called *In a Boat* beyond the reach of their intelligence.

Naturally enough, Hilaire Belloc is strongly drawn to the almost violent simplicity of the ballad. Bishop Percy would not have enjoyed the theological and political atmosphere of *The Little Serving Maid*, but he would have acknowledged its irresistible charm. There is that wholly delightful poem *The Death and Last Confession of Wandering Peter*—a most Bellocian vagabond. "He wandered everywhere he would: and all that he approved was sung, and most of what he saw was good." Says Peter:

"If all that I have loved and seen

Be with me on the Judgment Day,

I shall be saved the crowd between

From Satan and his foul array."

Hilaire Belloc has seen much and loved much. He has sung lustily the things he approved—with what hearty hatred has he sung the things he disapproved!

V

Hilaire Belloc is not the man to spend much time in analysing his own emotions; he is not, thank God, a poetical psychologist. Love songs, drinking songs, battle songs—it is with these primitive and democratic things that he is chiefly concerned.

But there is something more democratic than wine or love or war. That thing is Faith. And Hilaire Belloc's part in increasing the sum of the world's beauty would not be the considerable thing that it is were it not for his Faith. It is not that (like Dante Gabriel Rossetti) he is attracted by the Church's pageantry and wealth of legend. To Hilaire Belloc the pageantry is only incidental, the essential thing is his Catholic Faith. He writes convincingly about Our Lady and Saint Joseph and the Child Jesus because he himself is convinced. He does not delve into mediæval tradition in quest of picturesque incidents, he merely writes what he knows to be true. His Faith furnishes him with the theme for those of his poems which are most likely to endure; his Faith gives him the "rapture of an inspiration." His Faith enables him, as it has enabled many another poet, to see "in the lamp that is beauty, the light that is God."

And therein is Hilaire Belloc most thoroughly and consistently a democrat. For in this twentieth century it happens that there is on earth only one genuine democratic institution. And that institution is the Catholic Church.

TO DIVES

DIVES, when you and I go down to Hell,
Where scribblers end and millionaires as well,
We shall be carrying on our separate backs
Two very large but very different packs;
And as you stagger under yours, my friend,
Down the dull shore where all our journeys end,
And go before me (as your rank demands)
Towards the infinite flat underlands,
And that dear river of forgetfulness—
Charon, a man of exquisite address
(For, as your wife's progenitors could tell,
They're very strict on etiquette in Hell),
Will, since you are a lord, observe, "My lord,
We cannot take these weighty things aboard!"
Then down they go, my wretched Dives, down—
The fifteen sorts of boots you kept for town,
The hat to meet the Devil in; the plain
But costly ties; the cases of champagne;
The solid watch, and seal, and chain, and charm;
The working model of a Burning Farm

(To give the little Belials); all the three
Biscuits for Cerberus; the guarantee
From Lambeth that the Rich can never burn,
And even promising a safe return;
The admirable overcoat, designed
To cross Cocytus—very warmly lined:
Sweet Dives, you will leave them all behind

And enter Hell as tattered and as bare
As was your father when he took the air
Behind a barrow-load in Leicester Square.
Then turned to me, and noting one that brings
With careless step a mist of shadowy things:
Laughter and memories, and a few regrets,
Some honour, and a quantity of debts,
A doubt or two of sorts, a trust in God,
And (what will seem to you extremely odd)
His father's granfer's father's father's name,
Unspoilt, untitled, even spelt the same;
Charon, who twenty thousand times before
Has ferried Poets to the ulterior shore,
Will estimate the weight I bear, and cry—
"Comrade!" (He has himself been known to try
His hand at Latin and Italian verse,
Much in the style of Virgil—only worse)

"We let such vain imaginaries pass!"
Then tell me, Dives, which will look the ass—
You, or myself? Or Charon? Who can tell?
They order things so damnably in Hell.

STANZAS WRITTEN ON BATTERSEA BRIDGE DURING A SOUTH-WESTERLY GALE

THE woods and downs have caught the mid-December,
The noisy woods and high sea-downs of home;
The wind has found me and I do remember
The strong scent of the foam.

Woods, darlings of my wandering feet, another
Possesses you, another treads the Down;
The South West Wind that was my elder brother
Has come to me in town.

The wind is shouting from the hills of morning,
I do remember and I will not stay.
I'll take the Hampton road without a warning
And get me clean away.

The Channel is up, the little seas are leaping,
The tide is making over Arun Bar;

And there's my boat, where all the rest are sleeping
And my companions are.

I'll board her, and apparel her, and I'll mount her,
My boat, that was the strongest friend to me—
That brought my boyhood to its first encounter
And taught me the wide sea.

Now shall I drive her, roaring hard a' weather,
Right for the salt and leave them all behind.
We'll quite forget the treacherous streets together

And find—or shall we find?

There is no Pilotry my soul relies on
Whereby to catch beneath my bended hand,
Faint and beloved along the extreme horizon
That unforgotten land.

We shall not round the granite piers and paven
To lie to wharves we know with canvas furled.
My little Boat, we shall not make the haven—
It is not of the world.

Somewhere of English forelands grandly guarded
It stands, but not for exiles, marked and clean;

Oh! not for us. A mist has risen and marred it:—
My youth lies in between.

So in this snare that holds me and appals me,
Where honour hardly lives nor loves remain,
The Sea compels me and my Country calls me,
But stronger things restrain.

———

England, to me that never have malingered,
Nor spoken falsely, nor your flattery used,
Nor even in my rightful garden lingered:—
What have you not refused?

———

THE SOUTH COUNTRY

WHEN I am living in the Midlands
That are sodden and unkind,
I light my lamp in the evening:
My work is left behind;
And the great hills of the South Country
Come back into my mind.

The great hills of the South Country
They stand along the sea;
And it's there walking in the high woods
That I could wish to be,
And the men that were boys when I was a boy
Walking along with me.

The men that live in North England
I saw them for a day:
Their hearts are set upon the waste fells,
Their skies are fast and grey;
From their castle-walls a man may see
The mountains far away.

The men that live in West England
They see the Severn strong,
A-rolling on rough water brown
Light aspen leaves along.
They have the secret of the Rocks,
And the oldest kind of song.

But the men that live in the South Country

Are the kindest and most wise,
They get their laughter from the loud surf,
And the faith in their happy eyes
Comes surely from our Sister the Spring
When over the sea she flies;
The violets suddenly bloom at her feet,
She blesses us with surprise.

I never get between the pines
But I smell the Sussex air;
Nor I never come on a belt of sand
But my home is there.
And along the sky the line of the Downs
So noble and so bare.

A lost thing could I never find,
Nor a broken thing mend:

And I fear I shall be all alone
When I get towards the end.
Who will there be to comfort me
Or who will be my friend?

I will gather and carefully make my friends
Of the men of the Sussex Weald,
They watch the stars from silent folds,
They stiffly plough the field.
By them and the God of the South Country
My poor soul shall be healed.

If I ever become a rich man,
Or if ever I grow to be old,

I will build a house with deep thatch
To shelter me from the cold,
And there shall the Sussex songs be sung
And the story of Sussex told.

I will hold my house in the high wood
Within a walk of the sea,
And the men that were boys when I was a boy
Shall sit and drink with me.

THE FANATIC

LAST night in Compton Street, Soho,
A man whom many of you know
Gave up the ghost at half past nine.
That evening he had been to dine
At Gressington's—an act unwise,
But not the cause of his demise.
The doctors all agree that he
Was touched with cardiac atrophy
Accelerated (more or less)
By lack of proper food, distress,
Uncleanliness, and loss of sleep.
He was a man that could not keep
His money (when he had the same)
Because of creditors who came
And took it from him; and he gave
So freely that he could not save.
But all the while a sort of whim
Persistently remained with him,
Half admirable, half absurd:
To keep his word, to keep his word....

By which he did not mean what you
And I would mean (of payments due
Or punctual rental of the Flat—
He was a deal too mad for that)
But—as he put it with a fine
Abandon, foolish or divine—
But "That great word which every man

Gave God before his life began."
It was a sacred word, he said,
Which comforted the pathless dead
And made God smile when it was shown
Unforfeited, before the Throne.
And this (he said) he meant to hold
In spite of debt, and hate, and cold;
And this (he said) he meant to show
As passport to the wards below.
He boasted of it and gave praise
To his own self through all his days.
He wrote a record to preserve
How steadfastly he did not swerve
From keeping it; how stiff he stood
Its guardian, and maintained it good.
He had two witnesses to swear
He kept it once in Berkeley Square.

(Where hardly anything survives)
And, through the loneliest of lives
He kept it clean, he kept it still,
Down to the last extremes of ill.
So when he died, of many friends
Who came in crowds from all the ends
Of London, that it might be known
They knew the man who died alone,
Some, who had thought his mood sublime
And sent him soup from time to time,
Said, "Well, you cannot make them fit

The world, and there's an end of it!"
But others, wondering at him, said:
"The man that kept his word is dead!"
Then angrily, a certain third
Cried, "Gentlemen, he kept his word.
And as a man whom beasts surround
Tumultuous, on a little mound
Stands Archer, for one dreadful hour,
Because a Man is borne to Power—
And still, to daunt the pack below,
Twangs the clear purpose of his bow,
Till overwhelmed he dares to fall:
So stood this bulwark of us all.

He kept his word as none but he
Could keep it, and as did not we.
And round him as he kept his word
To-day's diseased and faithless herd,
A moment loud, a moment strong,
But foul forever, rolled along."

NOËL

I

On a winter's night long time ago
(*The bells ring loud and the bells ring low*),
When high howled wind, and down fell snow
(Carillon, Carilla).
Saint Joseph he and Notre Dame,
Riding on an ass, full weary came
From Nazareth into Bethlehem.
And the small child Jesus smile on you.

II

And Bethlehem inn they stood before
(*The bells ring less and the bells ring more*),
The landlord bade them begone from his door
(Carillon, Carilla).
"Poor folk" (says he), "must lie where they may,
For the Duke of Jewry comes this way,
With all his train on a Christmas Day."
And the small child Jesus smile on you.

III

Poor folk that may my carol hear
(*The bells ring single and the bells ring clear*),
See! God's one child had hardest cheer!
(Carillon, Carilla).
Men grown hard on a Christmas morn;
The dumb beast by and a babe forlorn.

It was very, very cold when our Lord was born.

And the small child Jesus smile on you.

IV

Now these were Jews as Jews must be

(The bells ring merry and the bells ring free),

But Christian men in a band are we

(Carillon, Carilla).

Empty we go, and ill be-dight,

Singing Noël on a Winter's night.

Give us to sup by the warm firelight,

And the small child Jesus smile on you.

THE EARLY MORNING

THE moon on the one hand, the dawn on the other:

The moon is my sister, the dawn is my brother.

The moon on my left and the dawn on my right.

My brother, good morning: my sister, good night.

THE BIRDS

When Jesus Christ was four years old,
The angels brought Him toys of gold,
Which no man ever had bought or sold.

And yet with these He would not play.
He made Him small fowl out of clay,
And blessed them till they flew away:
Tu creasti Domine.

Jesus Christ, Thou child so wise,
Bless mine hands and fill mine eyes,
And bring my soul to Paradise.

OUR LORD AND OUR LADY

THEY warned Our Lady for the Child
That was Our blessed Lord,
And She took Him into the desert wild,
Over the camel's ford.

And a long song She sang to Him
And a short story told:
And She wrapped Him in a woollen cloak
To keep Him from the cold.

But when Our Lord was grown a man
The Rich they dragged Him down,
And they crucified Him in Golgotha,
Out and beyond the Town.

They crucified Him on Calvary,
Upon an April day;
And because He had been her little Son
She followed Him all the way.

Our Lady stood beside the Cross,
A little space apart,

And when She heard Our Lord cry out
A sword went through Her Heart.

They laid Our Lord in a marble tomb,
Dead, in a winding sheet.
But Our Lady stands above the world
With the white Moon at Her feet.

IN A BOAT

LADY! Lady!
Upon Heaven-height,
Above the harsh morning
In the mere light.

Above the spindrift
And above the snow,
Where no seas tumble,
And no winds blow.

The twisting tides,
And the perilous sands
Upon all sides
Are in your holy hands.

The wind harries
And the cold kills;
But I see your chapel
Over far hills.

My body is frozen,
My soul is afraid:

Stretch out your hands to me,
Mother and maid.

Mother of Christ,
And Mother of me,
Save me alive
From the howl of the sea.

If you will Mother me

Till I grow old,

I will hang in your chapel

A ship of pure gold.

COURTESY

OF Courtesy, it is much less
Than Courage of Heart or Holiness,
Yet in my Walks it seems to me
That the Grace of God is in Courtesy.

On Monks I did in Storrington fall,
They took me straight into their Hall;
I saw Three Pictures on a wall,
And Courtesy was in them all.

The first the Annunciation;
The second the Visitation;
The third the Consolation,
Of God that was Our Lady's Son.

The first was of Saint Gabriel;
On Wings a-flame from Heaven he fell;
And as he went upon one knee
He shone with Heavenly Courtesy.

Our Lady out of Nazareth rode—
It was Her month of heavy load;
Yet was Her face both great and kind,
For Courtesy was in Her Mind.

The third it was our Little Lord,
Whom all the Kings in arms adored;
He was so small you could not see
His large intent of Courtesy.

Our Lord, that was Our Lady's Son,

Go bless you, People, one by one;

My Rhyme is written, my work is done.

THE NIGHT

MOST holy Night, that still dost keep
The keys of all the doors of sleep,
To me when my tired eyelids close
Give thou repose.

And let the far lament of them
That chaunt the dead day's requiem
Make in my ears, who wakeful lie,
Soft lullaby.

Let them that guard the horned moon
By my bedside their memories croon.
So shall I have new dreams and blest
In my brief rest.

Fold your great wings about my face,
Hide dawning from my resting-place,
And cheat me with your false delight,
Most Holy Night.

THE LEADER

THE sword fell down: I heard a knell;
I thought that ease was best,
And sullen men that buy and sell
Were host: and I was guest.
All unashamed I sat with swine,
We shook the dice for war,
The night was drunk with an evil wine—
But she went on before.

She rode a steed of the sea-foam breed,
All faery was her blade,
And the armour on her tender limbs
Was of the moonshine made.

By God that sends the master-maids,
I know not whence she came,
But the sword she bore to save the soul
Went up like an altar flame
Where a broken race in a desert place
Call on the Holy Name.

We strained our eyes in the dim day-rise,

We could not see them plain;
But two dead men from Valmy fen
Rode at her bridle-rein.

I hear them all, my fathers call,
I see them how they ride,
And where had been that rout obscene

Was an army straight with pride.
A hundred thousand marching men,
Of squadrons twenty score,
And after them all the guns, the guns,
But she went on before.

Her face was like a king's command
When all the swords are drawn.
She stretched her arms and smiled at us,
Her head was higher than the hills.
She led us to the endless plains.
We lost her in the dawn.

A BIVOUAC

I

YOU came without a human sound,
You came and brought my soul to me;
I only woke, and all around
They slumbered on the firelit ground,
Beside the guns in Burgundy.

II

I felt the gesture of your hands,
You signed my forehead with the Cross;
The gesture of your holy hands
Was bounteous—like the misty lands
Along the Hills in Calvados.

III

But when I slept I saw your eyes,
Hungry as death, and very far.
I saw demand in your dim eyes
Mysterious as the moons that rise
At midnight, in the Pines of Var.

TO THE BALLIOL MEN STILL IN AFRICA

YEARS ago when I was at Balliol,
Balliol men—and I was one—
Swam together in winter rivers,
Wrestled together under the sun.
And still in the heart of us, Balliol, Balliol,
Loved already, but hardly known,
Welded us each of us into the others:
Called a levy and chose her own.

Here is a House that armours a man
With the eyes of a boy and the heart of a ranger,
And a laughing way in the teeth of the world
And a holy hunger and thirst for danger:
Balliol made me, Balliol fed me,
Whatever I had she gave me again:
And the best of Balliol loved and led me.
God be with you, Balliol men.

I have said it before, and I say it again,
There was treason done, and a false word spoken,

And England under the dregs of men,
And bribes about, and a treaty broken:

But angry, lonely, hating it still,
I wished to be there in spite of the wrong.
My heart was heavy for Cumnor Hill
And the hammer of galloping all day long.

Galloping outward into the weather,

- 33 -

Hands a-ready and battle in all:
Words together and wine together
And song together in Balliol Hall.
Rare and single! Noble and few!...
Oh! they have wasted you over the sea!
The only brothers ever I knew,
The men that laughed and quarrelled with me.

Balliol made me, Balliol fed me,
Whatever I had she gave me again;
And the best of Balliol loved and led me,
God be with you, Balliol men.

VERSES TO A LORD

WHO, IN THE HOUSE OF LORDS, SAID THAT
THOSE WHO OPPOSED THE SOUTH AFRICAN
ADVENTURE CONFUSED SOLDIERS
WITH MONEY-GRUBBERS

YOU thought because we held, my lord,
An ancient cause and strong,
That therefore we maligned the sword:
My lord, you did us wrong.

We also know the sacred height
Up on Tugela side,
Where those three hundred fought with Beit
And fair young Wernher died.

The daybreak on the failing force,
The final sabres drawn:
Tall Goltman, silent on his horse,
Superb against the dawn.

The little mound where Eckstein stood
And gallant Albu fell,
And Oppenheim, half blind with blood,
Went fording through the rising flood—
My Lord, we know them well.

The little empty homes forlorn,
The ruined synagogues that mourn,
In Frankfort and Berlin;
We knew them when the peace was torn—
We of a nobler lineage born—

And now by all the gods of scorn

We mean to rub them in.

THE REBEL

THERE is a wall of which the stones
Are lies and bribes and dead men's bones.
And wrongfully this evil wall
Denies what all men made for all,
And shamelessly this wall surrounds
Our homesteads and our native grounds.

But I will gather and I will ride,
And I will summon a countryside,
And many a man shall hear my halloa
Who never had thought the horn to follow;
And many a man shall ride with me
Who never had thought on earth to see
High Justice in her armoury.

When we find them where they stand,
A mile of men on either hand,
I mean to charge from right away
And force the flanks of their array,
And press them inward from the plains,
And drive them clamouring down the lanes,

And gallop and harry and have them down,
And carry the gates and hold the town.
Then shall I rest me from my ride
With my great anger satisfied.

Only, before I eat and drink,
When I have killed them all, I think
That I will batter their carven names,

And slit the pictures in their frames,

And burn for scent their cedar door,

And melt the gold their women wore,

And hack their horses at the knees,

And hew to death their timber trees,

And plough their gardens deep and through—

And all these things I mean to do

For fear perhaps my little son

Should break his hands, as I have done.

THE PROPHET LOST IN THE HILLS
AT EVENING

STRONG God which made the topmost stars
To circulate and keep their course,
Remember me; whom all the bars
Of sense and dreadful fate enforce.

Above me in your heights and tall,
Impassable the summits freeze,
Below the haunted waters call
Impassable beyond the trees.

I hunger and I have no bread.
My gourd is empty of the wine.
Surely the footsteps of the dead
Are shuffling softly close to mine!

It darkens. I have lost the ford.
There is a change on all things made.
The rocks have evil faces, Lord,
And I am awfully afraid.

Remember me! the Voids of Hell
Expand enormous all around.
Strong friend of souls, Emmanuel,
Redeem me from accursed ground.

The long descent of wasted days,
To these at last have led me down;
Remember that I filled with praise
The meaningless and doubtful ways

That lead to an eternal town.

I challenged and I kept the Faith,
The bleeding path alone I trod;
It darkens. Stand about my wraith,
And harbour me—almighty God!

SONG

INVITING THE INFLUENCE OF A YOUNG LADY
UPON THE OPENING YEAR

I

YOU wear the morning like your dress
And are with mastery crowned;
Whenas you walk your loveliness
Goes shining all around.
Upon your secret, smiling way
Such new contents were found,
The Dancing Loves made holiday
On that delightful ground.

II

Then summon April forth, and send
Commandment through the flowers;
About our woods your grace extend
A queen of careless hours.
For oh, not Vera veiled in rain,
Nor Dian's sacred Ring,
With all her royal nymphs in train
Could so lead on the Spring.

THE RING

WHEN I was flying before the King
In the wood of Valognes in my hiding,
Although I had not anything
I sent a woman a golden ring.

A Ring of the Moors beyond Leon
With emerald and with diamond stone,
And a writing no man ever had known,
And an opal standing all alone.

The shape of the ring the heart to bind:
The emerald turns from cold to kind:
The writing makes her sure to find:—
But the evil opal changed her mind.

Now when the King was dead, was he,
I came back hurriedly over the sea
From the long rocks in Normandy
To Bosham that is by Selsey.
And we clipt each other knee to knee.
But what I had was lost to me.

CUCKOO!

IN woods so long time bare.

Cuckoo!

Up and in the wood, I know not where

Two notes fall.

Yet I do not envy him at all

His phantasy.

Cuckoo!

I too,

Somewhere,

I have sung as merrily as he

Who can dare,

Small and careless lover, so to laugh at care,

And who

Can call

Cuckoo!

In woods of winter weary,

In scented woods, of winter weary, call

Cuckoo!

In woods so long time bare.

THE MIRROR

THE mirror held your Fair, my Fair,
A fickle moment's space;
You looked into mine eyes and there
For ever fixed your face.

Keep rather to your Looking Glass
Than my more faithful eyes.
It told the truth. Alas! my lass!
My constant memory lies.

THE LITTLE SERVING MAID

I

THERE was a Queen of England,
And a good Queen too.
She had a house in Powis Land
With the Severn running through;
And Men-folk and Women-folk
Apprenticed to a trade;
But the prettiest of all
Was a Little Serving Maid.

II

"Oh Madam, Queen of England!
Oh will you let me go!
For there's a Lad in London
And he would have it so.
And I would have it too, Madam,
And with him would I bide;
And he will be the Groom, Madam,
And I shall be the Bride!"

III

"Oh fie to you and shame to you,
You Little Serving Maid!
And are you not astonied?
And are you not afraid?
For never was it known
Since Yngelonde began

That a Little Serving Maid
Should go a-meeting of a man!"

IV

Then the Little Serving Maid
She went and laid her down,
With her cross and her bede,
In her new courting gown.
And she called in Mother Mary's name
And heavily she sighed:
"I think that I have come to shame!"
And after that she died.

V

The good Queen of England
Her women came and ran:
"The Little Serving Maid is dead
From loving of a man!"

Said the good Queen of England
"That is ill news to hear!
Take her out and shroud her,
And lay her on a bier."

VI

They laid her on a bier,
In the court-yard all;
Some came from Foresting,
And some came from Hall.
And Great Lords carried her,

And proud Priests prayed.

And that was the end

Of the Little Serving Maid.

THE END OF THE ROAD

In these boots and with this staff

Two hundred leaguers and a half

Walked I, went I, paced I, tripped I,

Marched I, held I, skelped I, slipped I,

Pushed I, panted, swung and dashed I;

Picked I, forded, swam and splashed I,

Strolled I, climbed I, crawled and scrambled,

Dropped and dipped I, ranged and rambled;

Plodded I, hobbled I, trudged and tramped I,

And in lonely spinnies camped I,

And in haunted pinewoods slept I,

Lingered, loitered, limped and crept I,

Clambered, halted, stepped and leapt I;

Slowly sauntered, roundly strode I,

And ... (Oh! Patron saints and Angels

That protect the four Evangels!

And you Prophets vel majores

Vel incerti, vel minores,

Virgines ac confessores

Chief of whose peculiar glories

Est in Aula Regis stare

Atque orare et exorare

Et clamare et conclamare

Clamantes cum clamoribus

Pro Nobis Peccatoribus.)

Let me not conceal it.... *Rode I.*

(For who but critics could complain

Of "riding" in a railway train?)
Across the valley and the high-land,
With all the world on either hand
Drinking when I had a mind to,
Singing when I felt inclined to;
Nor ever turned my face to home
Till I had slaked my heart at Rome.

AUVERGNAT

THERE was a man was half a clown
(It's so my father tells of it).
He saw the church in Clermont town
And laughed to hear the bells of it.

He laughed to hear the bells that ring
In Clermont Church and round of it;
He heard the verger's daughter sing,
And loved her for the sound of it.

The verger's daughter said him nay;
She had the right of choice in it.
He left the town at break of day:
He hadn't had a voice in it.

The road went up, the road went down,
And there the matter ended it.
He broke his heart in Clermont town,
At Pontgibaud they mended it.

DRINKING SONG

ON THE EXCELLENCE OF BURGUNDY WINE

MY jolly fat host with your face all a-grin,

Come, open the door to us, let us come in.

A score of stout fellows who think it no sin

If they toast till they're hoarse, and they drink till they spin,

Hoofed it amain,

Rain or no rain,

To crack your old jokes, and your bottles to drain.

Such a warmth in the belly that nectar begets

As soon as his guts with its humour he wets,

The miser his gold, and the student his debts,

And the beggar his rags and his hunger forgets.

For there's never a wine

Like this tipple of thine

From the great hill of Nuits to the River of Rhine.

Outside you may hear the great gusts as they go

By Foy, by Duerne, and the hills of Lerraulx,

But the rain he may rain, and the wind he may blow,

If the Devil's above there's good liquor below.

So it abound,

Pass it around,

Burgundy's Burgundy all the year round.

DRINKING DIRGE

A THOUSAND years ago I used to dine
In houses where they gave me such regale
Of dear companionship and comrades fine
That out I went alone beyond the pale;
And riding, laughed and dared the skies malign
To show me all the undiscovered tale—
But my philosophy's no more divine,
I put my pleasure in a pint of ale.

And you, my friends, oh! pleasant friends of mine,
Who leave me now alone, without avail,
On Californian hills you gave me wine,
You gave me cider-drink in Longuevaille;
If after many years you come to pine
For comradeship that is an ancient tale—
You'll find me drinking beer in Dead Man's Chine.
I put my pleasure in a pint of ale.

In many a briny boat I've tried the brine,
From many a hidden harbour I've set sail,
Steering towards the sunset where there shine
The distant amethystine islands pale.

There are no ports beyond the far sea-line,
Nor any halloa to meet the mariner's hail;
I stand at home and slip the anchor-line.
I put my pleasure in a pint of ale.

ENVOI

Prince! Is it true when you go out to dine
You bring your bottle in a freezing pail?
Why then you cannot be a friend of mine.
I put my pleasure in a pint of ale.

WEST SUSSEX DRINKING SONG

THEY sell good Beer at Haslemere
And under Guildford Hill.
At Little Cowfold as I've been told
A beggar may drink his fill:
There is a good brew in Amberley too,
And by the bridge also;
But the swipes they take in at Washington Inn
Is the very best Beer I know.

Chorus

With my here it goes, there it goes,
All the fun's before us:
The Tipple's Aboard and the night is young,
The door's ajar and the Barrel is sprung,
I am singing the best song ever was sung
And it has a rousing chorus.

If I were what I never can be,
The master or the squire:
If you gave me the hundred from here to the sea,
Which is more than I desire:

Then all my crops should be barley and hops,
And did my harvest fail
I'd sell every rood of mine acres I would
For a belly-full of good Ale.

Chorus

With my here it goes, there it goes,

All the fun's before us:

The Tipple's aboard and the night is young,

The door's ajar and the Barrel is sprung,

I am singing the best song ever was sung

And it has a rousing chorus.

A BALLAD ON SOCIOLOGICAL
ECONOMICS

A WHILE ago it came to pass

(Merry we carol it all the day),

There sat a man on the top of an ass

(Heart be happy and carol be gay

In spite of the price of hay).

And over the down they hoofed it so

(Happy go lucky has best of fare),

The man up above and the brute below

(And singing we all forget to care

A man may laugh if he dare).

Over the stubble and round the crop

(Life is short and the world is round),

The donkey beneath and the man on top

(Oh! let good ale be found, be found,

Merry good ale and sound).

It happened again as it happened before

(Tobacco's a boon but ale is bliss),

The moke in the ditch and the man on the floor

(And that is the moral to this, to this

Remarkable artifice).

AN ORACLE

THAT WARNED THE WRITER WHEN ON PILGRIMAGE

MATUTINUS adest ubi Vesper, et accipiens te

Saepe recusatum voces intelligit hospes

Rusticus ignotas notas, ac flumina tellus

Occupat—In sancto tum, tum, stans Aede caveto

Tonsuram Hirsuti Capitis, via namque pedestrem

Ferrea praeveniens cursum, peregrine, laborem

Pro pietate tua inceptum frustratur, amore

Antiqui Ritus alto sub Numine Romae.

Translation of the above:—

When early morning seems but eve

And they that still refuse receive:

When speech unknown men understand;

And floods are crossed upon dry land.

Within the Sacred Walls beware

The Shaven Head that boasts of Hair,

For when the road attains the rail

The Pilgrim's great attempt shall fail.

HERETICS ALL

HERETICS all, whoever you be,
In Tarbes or Nimes, or over the sea,
You never shall have good words from me.
Caritas non conturbat me.

But Catholic men that live upon wine
Are deep in the water, and frank, and fine;
Wherever I travel I find it so,
Benedicamus Domino.

On childing women that are forlorn,
And men that sweat in nothing but scorn:
That is on all that ever were born,
Miserere Domine.

To my poor self on my deathbed,
And all my dear companions dead,
Because of the love that I bore them,
Dona Eis Requiem.

THE DEATH AND LAST CONFESSION
OF WANDERING PETER

WHEN Peter Wanderwide was young
He wandered everywhere he would:
And all that he approved was sung,
And most of what he saw was good.

When Peter Wanderwide was thrown
By Death himself beyond Auxerre,
He chanted in heroic tone
To priests and people gathered there:

"If all that I have loved and seen
Be with me on the Judgment Day,
I shall be saved the crowd between
From Satan and his foul array.

"Almighty God will surely cry,
'St. Michael! Who is this that stands
With Ireland in his dubious eye,
And Perigord between his hands,

"'And on his arm the stirrup-thongs,
And in his gait the narrow seas,

And in his mouth Burgundian songs,
But in his heart the Pyrenees?'

"St. Michael then will answer right
(And not without angelic shame),
'I seem to know his face by sight:
I cannot recollect his name...?'

"St. Peter will befriend me then,
Because my name is Peter too:
'I know him for the best of men
That ever walloped barley brew.

"'And though I did not know him well
And though his soul were clogged with sin,
I hold the keys of Heaven and Hell.
Be welcome, noble Peterkin.'

"Then shall I spread my native wings
And tread secure the heavenly floor,
And tell the Blessed doubtful things
Of Val d'Aran and Perigord."

This was the last and solemn jest
Of weary Peter Wanderwide.
He spoke it with a failing zest,
And having spoken it, he died.

DEDICATORY ODE

I MEAN to write with all my strength
(It lately has been sadly waning),
A ballad of enormous length—
Some parts of which will need explaining.[1]

Because (unlike the bulk of men
Who write for fame or public ends),
I turn a lax and fluent pen
To talking of my private friends.[2]

For no one, in our long decline,
So dusty, spiteful and divided,
Had quite such pleasant friends as mine,
Or loved them half as much as I did.

The Freshman ambles down the High,
In love with everything he sees,
He notes the very Midland sky,
He sniffs a more than Midland breeze.

"Can this be Oxford? This the place?"
(He cries) "of which my father said
The tutoring was a damned disgrace,
The creed a mummery, stuffed and dead?

"Can it be here that Uncle Paul
Was driven by excessive gloom,
To drink and debt, and, last of all,
To smoking opium in his room?

"Is it from here the people come,
Who talk so loud, and roll their eyes,
And stammer? How extremely rum!
How curious! What a great surprise.

"Some influence of a nobler day
Than theirs (I mean than Uncle Paul's),
Has roused the sleep of their decay,
And flecked with light their ancient walls.

"O! dear undaunted boys of old,
Would that your names were carven here,

For all the world in stamps of gold,
That I might read them and revere.

"Who wrought and handed down for me
This Oxford of the larger air,
Laughing, and full of faith, and free,
With youth resplendent everywhere?"

Then learn: thou ill-instructed, blind,
Young, callow, and untutored man,
Their private names were ...[3]
Their club was called REPUBLICAN.

Where on their banks of light they lie,
The happy hills of Heaven between,
The Gods that rule the morning sky
Are not more young, nor more serene

Than were the intrepid Four that stand,

The first who dared to live their dream.
And on this uncongenial land
To found the Abbey of Theleme.

We kept the Rabelaisian plan:[4]
We dignified the dainty cloisters
With Natural Law, the Rights of Man,
Song, Stoicism, Wine and Oysters.

The library was most inviting:
The books upon the crowded shelves
Were mainly of our private writing:
We kept a school and taught ourselves.

We taught the art of writing things
On men we still should like to throttle:
And where to get the Blood of Kings
At only half a crown a bottle.

Eheu Fugaces! Postume!
(An old quotation out of mode);
My coat of dreams is stolen away
My youth is passing down the road.

The wealth of youth, we spent it well
And decently, as very few can.
And is it lost? I cannot tell:
And what is more, I doubt if you can.

The question's very much too wide,
And much too deep, and much too hollow,
And learned men on either side
Use arguments I cannot follow.

They say that in the unchanging place,
Where all we loved is always dear,
We meet our morning face to face
And find at last our twentieth year....

They say (and I am glad they say)
It is so; and it may be so:
It may be just the other way,
I cannot tell. But this I know:

From quiet homes and first beginning,
Out to the undiscovered ends,
There's nothing worth the wear of winning,
But laughter and the love of friends.

But something dwindles, oh! my peers,
And something cheats the heart and passes,
And Tom that meant to shake the years
Has come to merely rattling glasses.

And He, the Father of the Flock,
Is keeping Burmesans in order,
An exile on a lonely rock
That overlooks the Chinese border.

And One (Myself I mean—no less),

Ah!—will Posterity believe it—
Not only don't deserve success,
But hasn't managed to achieve it.

Not even this peculiar town
Has ever fixed a friendship firmer,
But—one is married, one's gone down,
And one's a Don, and one's in Burmah.

And oh! the days, the days, the days,
When all the four were off together:
The infinite deep of summer haze,
The roaring charge of autumn weather!

I will not try the reach again,
I will not set my sail alone,
To moor a boat bereft of men
At Yarnton's tiny docks of stone.

But I will sit beside the fire,
And put my hand before my eyes,
And trace, to fill my heart's desire,
The last of all our Odysseys.

The quiet evening kept her tryst:
Beneath an open sky we rode,
And passed into a wandering mist
Along the perfect Evenlode.

The tender Evenlode that makes

Her meadows hush to hear the sound
Of waters mingling in the brakes,
And binds my heart to English ground.

A lovely river, all alone,
She lingers in the hills and holds
A hundred little towns of stones,
Forgotten in the western wolds

I dare to think (though meaner powers
Possess our thrones, and lesser wits
Are drinking worser wine than ours,
In what's no longer Austerlitz)

That surely a tremendous ghost,
The brazen-lunged, the bumper-filler,
Still sings to an immortal toast,
The Misadventures of the Miller.

The unending seas are hardly bar
To men with such a prepossession:
We were? Why then, by God, we *are*—
Order! I call the Club to session!

You do retain the song we set,
And how it rises, trips and scans?
You keep the sacred memory yet,
Republicans? Republicans?

You know the way the words were hurled,
To break the worst of fortune's rub?

I give the toast across the world,

And drink it, "Gentlemen: the Club."

FOOTNOTES:

[1]

But do not think I shall explain
To any great extent. Believe me,
I partly write to give you pain,
And if you do not like me, leave me.

[2]

And least of all can you complain,
Reviewers, whose unholy trade is,
To puff with all your might and main
Biographers of single ladies.

[3] Never mind.

[4]

The plan forgot (I know not how,
Perhaps the Refectory filled it),
To put a chapel in; and now
We're mortgaging the rest to build it.

DEDICATION ON THE GIFT OF A
BOOK TO A CHILD

CHILD! do not throw this book about!

Refrain from the unholy pleasure

Of cutting all the pictures out!

Preserve it as your chiefest treasure.

Child, have you never heard it said

That you are heir to all the ages?

Why, then, your hands were never made

To tear these beautiful thick pages!

Your little hands were made to take

The better things and leave the worse ones:

They also may be used to shake

The Massive Paws of Elder Persons.

And when your prayers complete the day,

Darling, your little tiny hands

Were also made, I think, to pray

For men that lose their fairylands.

DEDICATION OF A CHILD'S BOOK
OF IMAGINARY TALES

WHEREIN WRONG-DOERS SUFFER

AND is it true? It is not true!

And if it was it wouldn't do

For people such as me and you,

Who very nearly all day long

Are doing something rather wrong.

HOMAGE

I

THERE is a light around your head
Which only Saints of God may wear,
And all the flowers on which you tread
In pleasaunce more than ours have fed,
And supped the essential air
Whose summer is a-pulse with music everywhere.

II

For you are younger than the mornings are
That in the mountains break;
When upland shepherds see their only star
Pale on the dawn, and make
In his surcease the hours,
The early hours of all their happy circuit take.

FILLE-LA-HAINE

DEATH went into the steeple to ring,
And he pulled the rope and he tolled a knell.
Fille-la-Haine, how well you sing!
Why are they ringing the Passing Bell?
Death went into the steeple to ring;
Fille-la-Haine, how well you sing!

Death went down the stream in a boat,
Down the river of Seine went he;
Fille-la-Haine had a pain in her throat,
Fille-la-Haine was nothing to me.
Death went down the stream in a boat;
Fille-la-Haine had a pain in her throat.

Death went up the hill in a cart
(I have forgotten her lips and her laughter).
Fille-la-Haine was my sweetheart
(And all the village was following after).
Death went up the hill in a cart.
Fille-la-Haine was my sweetheart.

THE MOON'S FUNERAL

I

THE Moon is dead. I saw her die.
She in a drifting cloud was drest,
She lay along the uncertain west,
A dream to see.
And very low she spake to me:
"I go where none may understand,
I fade into the nameless land,
And there must lie perpetually."
And therefore I,
And therefore loudly, loudly I
And high
And very piteously make cry:
"The Moon is dead. I saw her die."

II

And will she never rise again?
The Holy Moon? Oh, never more!
Perhaps along the inhuman shore
Where pale ghosts are

Beyond the low lethean fen
She and some wide infernal star—
To us who loved her never more,
The Moon will never rise again.
Oh! never more in nightly sky
Her eye so high shall peep and pry
To see the great world rolling by.

For why?

The Moon is dead. I saw her die.

THE HAPPY JOURNALIST

I LOVE to walk about at night
By nasty lanes and corners foul,
All shielded from the unfriendly light
And independent as the owl.

By dirty grates I love to lurk;
I often stoop to take a squint
At printers working at their work.
I muse upon the rot they print.

The beggars please me, and the mud:
The editors beneath their lamps
As—Mr. Howl demanding blood,
And Lord Retender stealing stamps,

And Mr. Bing instructing liars,
His elder son composing trash;
Beaufort (whose real name is Meyers)
Refusing anything but cash.

I like to think of Mr. Meyers,
I like to think of Mr. Bing.
I like to think about the liars:
It pleases me, that sort of thing.

Policemen speak to me, but I,
Remembering my civic rights,
Neglect them and do not reply.
I love to walk about at nights!

At twenty-five to four I bunch

Across a cab I can't afford.

I ring for breakfast after lunch.

I am as happy as a lord!

LINES TO A DON

REMOTE and ineffectual Don
That dared attack my Chesterton,
With that poor weapon, half-impelled,
Unlearnt, unsteady, hardly held,
Unworthy for a tilt with men—
Your quavering and corroded pen;
Don poor at Bed and worse at Table,
Don pinched, Don starved, Don miserable;
Don stuttering, Don with roving eyes,
Don nervous, Don of crudities;
Don clerical, Don ordinary,
Don self-absorbed and solitary;
Don here-and-there, Don epileptic;
Don puffed and empty, Don dyspeptic;
Don middle-class, Don sycophantic,
Don dull, Don brutish, Don pedantic;
Don hypocritical, Don bad,
Don furtive, Don three-quarters mad;
Don (since a man must make an end),
Don that shall never be my friend.

Don different from those regal Dons!
With hearts of gold and lungs of bronze,
Who shout and bang and roar and bawl
The Absolute across the hall,
Or sail in amply bellowing gown

Enormous through the Sacred Town,
Bearing from College to their homes
Deep cargoes of gigantic tomes;
Dons admirable! Dons of Might!
Uprising on my inward sight
Compact of ancient tales, and port
And sleep—and learning of a sort.
Dons English, worthy of the land;
Dons rooted; Dons that understand.
Good Dons perpetual that remain
A landmark, walling in the plain—
The horizon of my memories—
Like large and comfortable trees.

Don very much apart from these,
Thou scapegoat Don, thou Don devoted,
Don to thine own damnation quoted,
Perplexed to find thy trivial name
Reared in my verse to lasting shame.
Don dreadful, rasping Don and wearing,

Repulsive Don—Don past all bearing.
Don of the cold and doubtful breath,
Don despicable, Don of death;
Don nasty, skimpy, silent, level;
Don evil; Don that serves the devil.
Don ugly—that makes fifty lines.
There is a Canon which confines
A Rhymed Octosyllabic Curse

If written in Iambic Verse
To fifty lines. I never cut;
I far prefer to end it—but
Believe me I shall soon return.
My fires are banked, yet still they burn
To write some more about the Don
That dared attack my Chesterton.

NEWDIGATE POEM

A PRIZE POEM SUBMITTED BY MR. LAMBKIN OF BURFORD TO THE EXAMINERS OF THE UNIVERSITY OF OXFORD ON THE PRESCRIBED POETIC THEME SET BY THEM IN 1893, "THE BENEFITS OF THE ELECTRIC LIGHT"

HAIL, Happy Muse, and touch the tuneful string!

The benefits conferred by Science[1] I sing.

Under the kind Examiners' direction[2]

I only write about them in connection

With benefits which the Electric Light

Confers on us; especially at night.

These are my theme, of these my song shall rise.

My lofty head shall swell to strike the skies.[3]

And tears of hopeless love bedew the maiden's eyes.

Descend, O Muse, from thy divine abode,

To Osney, on the Seven Bridges Road;

For under Osney's solitary shade

The bulk of the Electric Light is made.

Here are the works;—from hence the current flows

Which (so the Company's prospectus goes)

Can furnish to Subscribers hour by hour

No less than sixteen thousand candle power,[4]

All at a thousand volts. (It is essential

To keep the current at this high potential

In spite of the considerable expense.)

The Energy developed represents,

Expressed in foot-tons, the united forces

Of fifteen elephants and forty horses.
But shall my scientific detail thus
Clip the dear wings of Buoyant Pegasus?
Shall pure statistics jar upon the ear
That pants for Lyric accents loud and clear?
Shall I describe the complex Dynamo
Or write about its Commutator? No!
To happier fields I lead my wanton pen,
The proper study of mankind is men.
Awake, my Muse! Portray the pleasing sight

That meets us where they make Electric Light.
Behold the Electrician where he stands:
Soot, oil, and verdigris are on his hands;
Large spots of grease defile his dirty clothes,
The while his conversation drips with oaths.
Shall such a being perish in its youth?
Alas! it is indeed the fatal truth.
In that dull brain, beneath that hair unkempt,
Familiarity has bred contempt.
We warn him of the gesture all too late:
Oh, Heartless Jove! Oh, Adamantine Fate!
Some random touch—a hand's imprudent slip—
The Terminals—a flash—a sound like "Zip!"
A smell of burning fills the started Air—
The Electrician is no longer there!
But let us turn with true Artistic scorn
From facts funereal and from views forlorn
Of Erebus and Blackest midnight born.[5]

Arouse thee, Muse! and chaunt in accents rich
The interesting processes by which
The Electricity is passed along:
These are my theme: to these I bend my song.
It runs encased in wood or porous brick
Through copper wires two millimetres thick,
And insulated on their dangerous mission

By indiarubber, silk, or composition.
Here you may put with critical felicity
The following question: "What is Electricity?"
"Molecular Activity," say some,
Others when asked say nothing, and are dumb.
Whatever be its nature, this is clear:
The rapid current checked in its career,
Baulked in its race and halted in its course[6]
Transforms to heat and light its latent force:
It needs no pedant in the lecturer's chair
To prove that light and heat are present there.
The pear-shaped vacuum globe, I understand,
Is far too hot to fondle with the hand.
While, as is patent to the meanest sight,
The carbon filament is very bright.
As for the lights they hang about the town,
Some praise them highly, others run them down.
This system (technically called the Arc),
Makes some passages too light, others too dark.
But in the house the soft and constant rays
Have always met with universal praise.

For instance: if you want to read in bed
No candle burns beside your curtain's head,
Far from some distant corner of the room
The incandescent lamp dispels the gloom,
And with the largest print need hardly try
The powers of any young and vigorous eye.
Aroint thee, Muse! Inspired the poet sings!
I cannot help observing future things!
Life is a vale, its paths are dark and rough
Only because we do not know enough:
When Science has discovered something more
We shall be happier than we were before.
Hail, Britain, Mistress of the Azure Main,
Ten thousand Fleets sweep over thee in vain!
Hail, Mighty Mother of the Brave and Free,
That beat Napoleon, and gave birth to me!
Thou that canst wrap in thine emblazoned robe
One quarter of the habitable globe.
Thy mountains, wafted by a favouring breeze,
Like mighty rocks withstand the stormy seas.
Thou art a Christian Commonwealth; and yet
Be thou not all unthankful—nor forget
As thou exultest in Imperial Might
The Benefits of the Electric Light.

FOOTNOTES:

[1] To be pronounced as a monosyllable in the Imperial fashion.

[2] Mr. Punt, Mr. Howl, and Mr. Grewcock (now, alas, deceased).

[3] A neat rendering of "Sublimi feriam sidera vertice."

[4] To the Examiners: These facts (of which I guarantee the accuracy) were given me by a Director.

[5] A reminiscence of Milton: "Fas est et ab hoste doceri."

[6] Lambkin told me he regretted this line, which was for the sake of Rhyme. He would willingly have replaced it, but to his last day could construct no substitute.

THE YELLOW MUSTARD

OH! ye that prink it to and fro,
In pointed flounce and furbelow,
What have ye known, what can ye know
That have not seen the mustard grow?

The yellow mustard is no less
Than God's good gift to loneliness;
And he was sent in gorgeous press
To jangle keys at my distress.

I heard the throstle call again,
Come hither, Pain! come hither, Pain!
Till all my shameless feet were fain
To wander through the summer rain.

And far apart from human place,
And flaming like a vast disgrace,
There struck me blinding in the face
The livery of the mustard race.

———————————

To see the yellow mustard grow
Beyond the town, above, below;
Beyond the purple houses, oh!
To see the yellow mustard grow!

———————————

ON HYGIENE

OF old when folk lay sick and sorely tried,

The doctors gave them medicine and they died.

Here is an happier age, for now we know

Both how to make men sick and keep them so.

THE FALSE HEART

I SAID to Heart, "How goes it?" Heart replied:
"Right as a Ribstone Pippin!" But it lied.

A critic said large margins did not please him,
I therefore printed just two lines, to tease him.
And if he still complains of what I've done,
In my next book I'll fill a page with ONE.

SONNET UPON GOD, THE WINE GIVER

(For Easter Sunday)

THOUGHT Man made wine, I think God made it, too;

God making all things, made Man made good wine.

He taught him how the little tendrils twine

About the stakes of labor close and true.

Then next, with intimate prophetic laughter,

He taught the Man, in His own image blest,

To pluck and wagon and to—all the rest!

To tread the grape and work his vintage after.

So did God make us, making good wine makers;

So did He order us to rule the field

And now by God are we not only bakers;

But winners also sacraments to yield;

Yet most of all strong lovers, Praised be God!

Who taught us how the wine-press should be trod!

THE POLITICIAN
OR THE IRISH EARLDOM

A STRONG and striking Personality,
Worth several hundred thousand pounds—
Of strict political Morality—
Was walking in his park-like Grounds;
When, just as these began to pall on him
(I mean the Trees, and Things like that),
A Person who had come to call on him
Approached him, taking off his Hat.

He said, with singular veracity:
"I serve our Sea-girt Mother-Land
In no conspicuous capacity.
I am but an Attorney; and
I do a little elementary
Negotiation, now and then,
As Agent for a Parliamentary
Division of the Town of N....

"Merely as one of the Electorate—
A member of the Commonweal—

Before completing my Directorate,
I want to know the way you feel
On matters more or less debatable;
As—whether our Imperial Pride
Can treat as taxable or rateable
The Gardens of ..." His host replied:

"The Ravages of Inebriety

(Alas! increasing day by day!)
Are undermining all Society.
I do not hesitate to say
My country squanders her abilities,
Observe how Montenegro treats
Her Educational Facilities....
... As to the African defeats,

"I bitterly deplored their frequency;
On Canada we are agreed,
The Laws protecting Public Decency
Are very, very lax indeed!
The Views of most of the Nobility
Are very much the same as mine,
On Thingumbob's eligibility ...
I trust that you remain to dine?"

His Lordship pressed with importunity,
As rarely he had pressed before.

It gave them both an opportunity
To know each other's value more.

SHORT BALLAD AND POSTSCRIPT ON CONSOLS

I

GIGANTIC daughter of the West
(The phrase is Tennysonian), who
From this unconquerable breast
The vigorous milk of Freedom drew
—We gave it freely—shall the crest
Of Empire in your keeping true,
Shall England—I forget the rest,
But Consols are at 82.

II

Now why should any one invest,
As even City people do
(His Lordship did among the rest),
When stocks—but what is that to you?
And then, who ever could have guessed
About the guns—and horses too!—
Besides, they knew their business best,
And Consols are at 82.

III

It serves no purpose to protest,
It isn't manners to halloo
About the way the thing was messed—
Or vaguely call a man a Jew.
A gentleman who cannot jest

Remarked that we should muddle through
(The continent was much impressed),
And Consols are at 82.

And, Botha lay at Pilgrim's Rest
And Myberg in the Great Karroo
(A desert to the south and west),
And Consols are at 82.

Postscript

Permit me—if you do not mind—
To add it would be screaming fun
If, after printing this, I find
Them after all at 81.

Or 70 or 63,
Or 55 or 44,
Or 39 and going free,
Or 28—or even more.

No matter—take no more advice
From doubtful and intriguing men.
Refuse the stuff at any price,
And slowly watch them fall to 10.

Meanwhile I feel a certain zest
In writing once again the new
Refrain that all is for the best,
And Consols are at 82.

Milton Keynes UK
Ingram Content Group UK Ltd.
UKHW032231011124
450424UK00008B/951

9 789362 928924